EVERY DAY
with Je
FOR GROWING CH

GETTING THE
BEST OUT OF THE
BIBLE

BY SELWYN HUGHES

QUIET TIME

God, look at me!
Confined to pages flipped
on the calendar
Stuck in a wear-dated body,
Trapped in a tongue-tied heart,
Bound on the ropes of repetition,
Trained on the leash of irritation,
Perimetered by fences of frustration,
Caught thrashing in the net
of humanity.
O limitless Lord!
Give me wings to soar above
the boundaries
Free in the boundless arms
of your love.

Susan L. Lenzkes
© by author

A TIME OF DISCOVERY!

For Reading and Meditation: Psalm 46:1–11

"Be still, and know that I am God ..." (v. 10)

We begin today to look at one of the most important subjects we could ever examine – Getting the best out of the Bible. The title suggests that there are those who do not get the best out of the Bible – and of this there can be no doubt. Many read the Bible, study the Bible, memorise the Bible, and yet fail to get the best out of it. And why? Because they miss the biggest single secret of making the Bible come alive in their life and experience – *meditation.*

A LOST ART

For some reason Bible meditation has largely been lost by the Church of this century and it desperately needs to be recovered. In an age of increasing uncertainty, the one sure way to maintain spiritual peace and poise is by meditating on God's Word daily. Many believers, however, view meditation as something practised by gurus, mystics or eastern religions, and look askance at those who advocate its usefulness in the Christian Church. David Ray, an American writer and minister, says, "I, for one, looked with suspicion on any Christian who advocated such a practice as meditation. I thought to myself, 'They are out of touch with reality. Give me action and work, lots of work. Let somebody else waste time staring at the end of his nose.'" Then someone introduced him to the principles of Bible meditation, showed him how to let Psalm 46:10 soak into his thoughts, and within days he became more aware of God's presence in his life than ever before. Focus your thoughts on this verse today, and resolve to make the coming days a time of spiritual discovery and development.

The one sure way to maintain spiritual peace.

O Father, help me as I begin this quest to know You better and be more aware of Your presence in my life. Grant in the coming days that all the clouds will part and I will see – really see. In Jesus' Name I pray. Amen.

THE WORD AND THE SPIRIT
For Reading and Meditation: Matthew 22:23–33

"… You are in error because you do not know the
Scriptures or the power of God." (v. 29)

I you are a Christian and you feel a need and a desire to increase your personal awareness of God, then one of the most effective ways of achieving that is through Biblical meditation. Notice I say *Bible* meditation, for there are many forms and many approaches to the subject of meditation which claim to lead people to God, but which, in fact, lead them away from him.

ONLY ONE WAY

The only way a person can know God is through a personal encounter with Jesus Christ. The glorious message of the Bible is summed up in the fact that when there was nothing we could do to climb up to God, the Almighty God came down to us. The Son of God became the Son of Man in order that the sons of men might become the sons of God.

The Bible is the only way through which Christians can increase their understanding and awareness of God. The verse before us today says, "You are in error because you do not know the Scriptures or the power of God." The way to keep from erring (and by inference to build up one's understanding and knowledge of God) is to know these two things – the Scriptures, (the past revelation) and the power of God.

Some only know the Scriptures – the past revelation – they do not link themselves with the power of the Holy Spirit who operates in the Word. They err, for they view the Word as a mere historic document. Others know the power of the Holy Spirit in their life and experience, but they do not know the Scriptures in any real sense. They too err – for we cannot correctly discern God at work in our lives and churches unless we continually check it by the revelation contained in the Scriptures.

The Almighty God came down to us.

Thank you, Father, that when I could not reach You through my highest thoughts, your thoughts discovered a way to reach me. And your highest thought is – Jesus.

TWO MEN – TWO METHODS

For Reading and Meditation: Psalm 63:1–11

"… my mouth shall praise thee … When I remember thee upon my bed, and meditate on thee …" (vs. 5–6, AV)

We are seeing that meditation, in order to be effective in increasing our personal awareness of God, must be directly related to the Bible. Dr Stanley Jones in one of his books says, "I know of a devoted Christian who comes to his Quiet Time without a Bible and just sits in meditation. He thinks he can come to God direct. But does he? He gets to God through the medium of his own conceptions of God. His conceptions are the medium. His conceptions are man's thoughts of God. So my friend is an unstable Christian. He is subject to his own moods. He is self-centred instead of Scripture-centred."

GOD'S THOUGHTS

We cannot expect to increase our personal awareness of God by simply communing with our own thoughts. Unless our thoughts are constantly corrected by God's thoughts, our thoughts will go off at a tangent or revolve around themselves. A traveller tells how once when travelling across the Atlantic on a passenger ship, he saw two men begin each day in different ways. One, a businessman, began his day by eagerly picking up the daily news-sheet and turning at once to the stock market report. His face took on the expression of what he saw there – if it was up, his countenance showed it, and if it was down, his face fell too. The other man, a Christian missionary, began his day differently. He leaned over the rail each morning reading his Bible – then looked out at the open sea in meditation. His face wore a calm expression. It was obvious that this man's happiness did not depend on what was happening, but on an awareness of God that was not subject to the changing circumstances of time.

Our thoughts will go off at a tangent.

O Father, help me to have Your Word hidden in my heart so deeply that it becomes the hidden springs of action, determining my character and my conduct in all of life's circumstances. In Jesus' Name I pray. Amen.

THE STARTING POINT

For Reading and Meditation: Philippians 2:1–11

"Who, being in very nature God, did not consider equality with God something to be grasped." (v. 6)

We ended Day 2 by saying that when there was nothing we could do to climb up to God, the Almighty God came down to us in the Person of His Son. This fact lies at the heart of the Bible and is the key to the opening of its treasures. Miss this and you miss the focal point of revelation.

GOD'S HIGHEST THOUGHT

The Bible progressively uncovers the nature of God as we are able to understand it, and the final and perfect revelation of God is seen in Jesus. The Incarnation is the revelation. Everything else develops from this point. Where the emphasis on the Incarnation is weak then the sense of revelation is weak, and people go off into all kinds of so-called "revelations" that amount to nothing more than fantasies. They discover "Christ within themselves" which turns out to be a Christ of their own creation. The lineaments of Jesus fade out and a Christ of sentimentalism takes His place. This is why there can be no room for transcendental meditation in the Christian Church.

If we try to build up our personalities from any other starting point than Jesus then we will be like those of whom it is described:

> *They sail away on a sea of mist*
> *To a land that doesn't exist.*

Pastor Robinson, one of the men who ministered to the Pilgrim Fathers, said, "Much light will yet break out from the Word of God, especially if the 'Word of God' is the Word of God – 'the Word made Flesh'." Transcendental meditation seeks to get its converts to empty their minds to find God. Christianity encourages its converts to fill their minds with God's thoughts. And again I say God's highest thought is – Jesus.

The final and perfect revelation of God is found in Jesus.

O Father, how true it is that the entrance of Your Word gives light. I read other books to get light; I read the Book to get the Light. Thank You, Father. Amen.

WHAT IS MEDITATION?

For Reading and Meditation: John 1:1–14

"The Word became flesh ..." (v. 14)

To get the best out of the Bible, we must be clear about its central message, which is the fact of the Incarnation. Some come to the Bible and use it as a book of magic out of which they pick magic formulas and magic facts. The Bible is not a magical revelation but a moral revelation. It shows us that in the Incarnation, God invades humanity with incorrigible love. We do not have to find God; we simply let God find us. Miss your way here and you come out with wrong conclusions about God, life and salvation. In receiving Jesus, we are one with God, and having been brought into a relationship with the Almighty through faith in His Son, we are then ready to increase our knowledge of the living Word through and by the written Word.

SPIRITUAL DIGESTION

Now it is time to ask ourselves: What exactly is meditation? Andrew Murray describes it as "holding the Word of God in your heart until it has affected every phase of your life". It is the art of contemplation, and close or continued thought. It is revolving a subject in the mind so that its many sides are reviewed. Someone else described it as like "gazing long at a prism of many facets, turning it from angle to angle in a bright spotlight". But perhaps the best definition of meditation is this: "It is the process by which we take the Word of God and turn it into spiritual faith and energy; taking Biblical principles and making them working realities." Meditation, therefore, is the digestive system of the soul. The man who only reads, studies and memorises the Bible but fails to meditate on it is like a man who chews his food but refuses to swallow it.

The art of contemplation.

Father, I sense that I am now coming to the crux of the matter. Help me to grasp clearly, the truth which I know You are seeking to teach me. In Jesus' Name. Amen.

ABSORBING CHRIST'S LIFE
For Reading and Meditation: John 15:1–16

*"... It is the man who shares my life and whose life
I share who proves fruitful ..." (v. 5, J B Phillips)*

We continue exploring the meaning of meditation. One of the synonyms for the word "meditate" is ruminate. Many animals, such as sheep, goats, antelope, camels, cows, and giraffe are called ruminant animals. This is because they have stomachs with several compartments – the first of which is called the rumen. The way a ruminant animal digests its food is fascinating. First, it literally bolts its food down, and then later it regurgitates the food out of its first stomach, the rumen, back into its mouth. This regurgitation process enables the food to be thoroughly digested, whereupon it is absorbed into the animal's bloodstream so becoming part of its life. Rumination and meditation are parallel words.

SPIRITUAL NOURISHMENT

When a Christian takes a thought from the Scriptures, and begins to meditate upon it, he actually passes that thought from his mind into his spirit, backwards and forwards, over and over again, until it is absorbed into his spiritual bloodstream and is translated into spiritual faith and energy. Just as a ruminant animal gets its nourishment and energy from the grass through regurgitation, so does a Christian extract from the Scriptures the life of Christ through meditation. Meditation on the Word of God transfers the life of Christ to every part of the Christian's personality. So remember, it is not enough simply to read the Bible, study the Bible or memorise the Bible. To extract from it the life of God which He has deposited in His Word, we must meditate upon it.

Translated into spiritual faith and energy.

O Father, I feel as if I am on the brink of one of the greatest discoveries of my life. I am eager to learn more. Take me by the hand and lead me to greater and deeper understanding. In Jesus' Name. Amen.

THE MEDITATION PROCESS

For Reading and Meditation: Psalm 4:1–8

"… commune with your own heart upon your bed, and be still." (v. 4, AV)

Reading the Bible, studying the Bible and memorising the Bible are primarily intellectual exercises which bring spiritual results. Meditation is not primarily an intellectual exercise, but a way by which the Word of God is carried direct into the spirit where it can accomplish its greatest work.

A SECOND THOUGHT

To understand what goes on in meditation, one must see the difference between the soul and the spirit. The Bible teaches that there are three parts to our being – spirit, soul and body (1 Thess. 5:23). It also teaches that there is a clear difference between the spirit and the soul (Heb 4:12; Luke 1:46–47). The spirit is the centre of our personality, the motivating point of our whole being. The Bible sometimes speaks of it as the "heart". The soul is that part of us which contains our mind (or thoughts), our feelings and our decisions. When we read, study and memorise the Bible, the action goes on in our minds and eventually passes into our spirits. When we meditate, however, we drop the Word of God instantly into our spirits so that it can achieve maximum effectiveness.

In our text for today, the Psalmist bids us to "commune with your own heart (or spirit) upon your bed". In this verse he clarifies what meditation is all about. It is passing the Word of God from the soul into the spirit – backwards and forwards, over and over again – so that its cleansing and therapeutic power permeates the whole of our personality.

To get the best out of life, great matters have to be given a second thought. Meditation is just that – giving Biblical truths a second thought.

We drop the Word of God instantly into our hearts.

O Father, anoint my eyes to see the truth that I am looking at today, for I know only too well that the natural mind understands not the things of God for they are spiritually discerned. For Jesus' sake. Amen.

FOCUSING ON GOD'S THOUGHTS

For Reading and Meditation: Proverbs 4:14–27

"Guard your heart, for it is the wellspring of life." (v. 23)

A s so much depends on a clear understanding of the meaning of meditation, we must spend another day discussing it. Meditation (as we have seen) is the spiritual exercise we go through when we hold a word, a thought or a verse of Scripture in our minds and then proceed to drop it into our spirits, bringing it back again into the mind, returning it to the spirit, backwards and forwards, over and over again, until we extract from it the very life of Christ which lies in His Word. Just as a cow chewing the cud brings it up into its mouth, lets it drop back into its stomach, and continues this process until every ounce of nourishment has been extracted, so in meditation, we pass the Word of God from our mind into our spirit, continuing this process until we have spiritually digested it.

THE UNSEEN SCULPTOR

I cannot emphasise enough that meditation is only beneficial when it focuses on God's thoughts – not on our thoughts. Beware of getting alone with your own thoughts. There is great danger in rummaging around in thoughts of the past – mistakes you made, romances that never turned out the way you expected, examinations you failed.

Put these thoughts behind you and concentrate on thinking God's thoughts after Him. Once you have grasped the concept of meditation and know how to apply it in your life, you will find your spirit becoming the secret workshop of an unseen Sculptor, chiselling in the secret chambers of your heart, the living forms that contribute to your character development, and make your life a radiant testimony to the power and grace of the Lord Jesus Christ.

A radiant testimony to ... the Lord Jesus Christ.

O Father, help me to focus more on Your thoughts than I do on my own, and help me to begin this way of life today. Amen.

MEDITATION BRINGS SUCCESS

For Reading and Meditation: Joshua 1:1–9

"... meditate on it day and night, ... Then you will be prosperous and successful." (v. 8)

Having considered over the past few days the meaning and import of the word meditation, we turn now to give our attention to its rewards and benefits. One of the first benefits that comes out of Biblical meditation, as seen in the passage before us today, is success.

THE SECRET

The book of Joshua narrates the story of how a man of proven character and ability, and one of only three adults to survive the 40 years of wilderness wandering, led a nation of several million people across the flood-swollen Jordan river to settle in their Promised Land. When God said, "Moses my servant is dead" (1:2) the reins of leadership passed to Joshua. And what a leader Joshua became. In a brilliant, divinely inspired move, he skilfully divided Canaan in half, then systematically defeated the southern armies before marching north to conquer the remaining occupants of the land. During the seven-year period this book covers, the 12 tribes met and defeated a total of 31 armies and captured 20 cities. What was the secret of Joshua's outstanding success? It was this – meditation. Meditate day and night and you will "be successful" (v. 8).

As Joshua meditated on God's Word, the continuous inner mental and spiritual discipline produced in him clarity of thought, sharpness of intellect and a greater power of concentration. There is no doubt (in my mind at least) that Joshua's success as a military leader stemmed directly from his willingness and ability to meditate in the Scriptures. And remember, Joshua had just a fragment of what is now available to you and me.

Spiritual discipline produced ... clarity of thought.

Heavenly Father, thank You for showing me that true success comes only when I learn to meditate on Your Word. Amen.

EXCELLING IN UNDERSTANDING
For Reading and Meditation: Psalm 119:97–104

"I have more insight than all my teachers, for I meditate on your statutes." (v. 99)

We saw yesterday that one of the benefits of meditating on the Word of God is true success. Today we examine another of those benefits – understanding. The understanding spoken of here is that special insight God gives to those who meditate on His Word, enabling them to discern more than the recognised authorities. The world gains its understanding of life through observation, experience and the acquiring of knowledge. The Christian who meditates, however, is given an inner awareness of the principles which guide and govern the moral universe. There are so many philosophies abroad today that unless we can see through the faulty structure of these systems and recognise them for what they are, we will never experience a happy and joyous life.

THE SCHOOL OF MEDITATION
Understanding has been defined as "the right application of knowledge". Much of the knowledge gained by today's society is directly contrary to God's eternal principles. The world, for example, believes that the way to greatness is to become a leader. God says differently. "But he that is greatest among you shall be your servant" (Matt. 23:11, AV).

Again, the world would reprove a scorner, but the Scripture points out that whilst it is necessary to reprove those who do wrong, a scorner should be left alone (Prov. 9:8). Whilst we must not be unmindful of the benefits of secular education, we must realise that whilst it ministers to the needs of the mind, it fails to minister to the needs of the spirit. But for those who are truly His, God has provided a "higher" education. In His school of meditation we gain more understanding than all our teachers.

God has provided a "higher" education.

Father, I begin to see the school as the framework in which my spirit can be educated. Help me to become a meditator as I make my enrolment in the school of "higher" education. Amen.

DISCERNING BETWEEN GOOD AND BAD

For Reading and Meditation: Psalm 119:9–16

*"I have hidden your word in my heart that
I might not sin against you." (v. 11)*

Another benefit of meditation is the ability to discern the difference between right and wrong. Our text for today makes that abundantly clear. "I have hidden your word in my heart that I might not sin against you." In 1 Kings 3:5 God appeared to Solomon and told him he could have whatever he wanted. And what was his request? "Give therefore thy servant an understanding heart ... that I may discern between good and bad" (v. 9, AV). God was greatly pleased with his request and gave him, in addition to wisdom and understanding, riches and honour. The ability to discern the difference between right and wrong is an important part of our spiritual development and comes about mainly through exposure to the Word of God.

When we read and meditate upon the Word of God, God uses the Word hidden in our hearts to show us when our thoughts, actions and attitudes are displeasing to Him.

SPIRITUAL FRUITFULNESS

One of the major reasons why so many Christians live barren and unfruitful lives is because they fail to meditate in the Scriptures. Psalm 1 explains that the secret of a spiritually fruitful life is to send one's roots down into the Word of God by meditation. As we do this we draw upon the life of God in His Word which in turn, produces the spiritual fruitfulness the Bible everywhere encourages us to reveal. The picture is of a tree planted by the river, bringing forth fruit in its season, and whose leaves never wither. Could your Christian life be described like that?

We draw upon the life of God in His Word.

O Father, more and more I am coming to see that Your life pulses through the very pages of this book, the Bible. Help me to tap that life and power daily. For Jesus' sake. Amen.

DISCOVER HOW TO LIVE

For Reading and Meditation: Proverbs 4:1–13

"... keep my commands and you will live." (v. 4)

We must spend one more day in examining the benefits of meditation. Over the past few days we have seen that when we meditate in the Scriptures, God promises we will be successful in everything we do, understand more than the recognised authorities, discern the difference between right and wrong, and become spiritually fruitful and prosperous. The verse before us today gives us yet another benefit of meditation – we discover how to live. We know everything about life except how to live it. The truth is that although we are truly converted Christians, we will never know how to live effectively until we learn to tap, through meditation, the resources of God which He has deposited in His Word, the Bible. It is true, of course, that we draw the life of God into our spirits through personal prayer, but prayer by itself is not enough – to live and live effectively, we must saturate our thoughts in the Word of our God. "Lay hold of my words with all your heart; keep my commands and you will live."

THE RIGHT COMBINATION

When we meditate on the Scriptures, we experience a heightening of all the powers of the personality, enabling us to gain a degree and quality of life which is divine.

The mind becomes keener and more creative, the emotions become broader and more sensitive, the will becomes more active and decisive.

That great statement of Augustine is often repeated because often corroborated: "Thou hast made us for thyself and our hearts are restless until they find their rest in thee." Let this fact be burned into your mind – meditation is the combination which gives you access to God's locked treasures of life and power.

We know everything about life except how to live it.

O Father, Your Word is becoming more and more my treasure. And where my treasure is, there is my heart also. Show me more so that I can not only experience the Abundant Life of which Your Word speaks, but also share it with others. Amen.

THE RIGHT TIME TO MEDITATE

For Reading and Meditation: Deuteronomy 6:1–9

"... when you sit at home and when you walk along the road, when you lie down and when you get up." (v. 7)

We must give some thought to the question of when to meditate. It must be fairly obvious that there are times when a Christian ought not to meditate. Those involved in tasks where the safety of others depends on their fullest concentration should not give their minds to meditation. It should also be emphasised that an employee, during working hours, should give his full and undivided attention to the task set him by his employer. However, there are some tasks which are so routine, it is possible to think of something else at the same time without detracting from one's efficiency. Although meditation is an important and God-ordained way of building up our spiritual lives, we must never forget that during the hours of employment, our employer must have our fullest and undivided attention.

ISLANDS OF SOLITUDE

The verse before us today spells out the four special occasions when meditation ought to be practised: (1) When you sit in your house – or during times of leisure and relaxation. Dr Alexis Carrel says, "We have lost the art in this modern age of developing 'islands of solitude'. No attempt has been made in the new towns and cities to build quiet isolated areas where meditation would be possible. Both the city and the home are impoverished without these 'islands of solitude'." (2) When you walk to and from work or school. You probably know every inch of that morning walk to work, to the station, to the bus stop or to school. Use the walk for an extra purpose – meditate. Select a verse of Scripture and do the same as the great C H Spurgeon. "Whenever I go for a walk," he said, "I take a verse of Scripture as I would a sweet on the end of my tongue, and suck every precious drop of sweetness from it."

Use the walk for an extra purpose – meditate.

Lord, forgive me for the minutes and hours I waste every day which could be utilised in building up my spiritual resources. Help me to be alert for every opportunity to meditate on Your Word. For Jesus' sake. Amen.

WEEK 2

DAY 6

FUEL FOR THE SUBCONSCIOUS
For Reading and Meditation: Proverbs 6:12–22

"... when you sleep, they will watch over you." (v. 22)

We continue looking at the proper times to meditate: (3) When you lie down before going to sleep at night. I have spoken before about the importance of holding God's Word in your mind immediately prior to going to sleep, but let me expand a little more on this today. Every night when we go to sleep, a marvellous transition takes place. The conscious mind hands over to the subconscious mind the responsibility of keeping everything under control. The subconscious mind knows full well what its task is – to rebuild the physical and mental parts of the body so that they are ready to begin another day. It does so by decelerating the heartbeat from a normal 72 beats per minute to 60 or less. If all goes according to plan we wake up the next morning refreshed and ready to begin another day.

THE NIGHT KEY
But what happens when the conscious mind transfers to the subconscious a deep or a pressing problem? A restless night might be in store. The subconscious mind doesn't want to handle negative fears and thoughts as these interfere with its ability to rejuvenate the system. Energy goes into fighting these thoughts and so we wake up tired and unrefreshed. But what happens when the subconscious mind is handed a portion of the Word of God? It delights in it; this is what it was made for.

Someone described it as "giving God the night key to our hearts". So go to sleep each night meditating on the Word of God, and you will find, taking place in your life and experience, the power of these tremendous words, "When you sleep, they will watch over you." Pleasant dreams!

Go to sleep each night meditating on the Word of God.

O Father, help me daily to put all my worries, frustrations, fears and anxieties into Your hands and give my subconscious mind the fuel it needs to function effectively – Your eternal and infallible Word. In Jesus' Name. Amen.

GOOD MORNING LORD!

For Reading and Meditation: Proverbs 6:22–35

*"… when you awake, they will speak
to you." (v. 22)*

We come now to the last of the four specific occasions when we should meditate. (4) When you rise up at the beginning of the day. If your last thought at night has been something from the Word of God, then when you wake up it will speak right back to you. What a way to begin a day! Learn to exploit the power of your subconscious to your advantage. It's going to work on something while you are asleep, so let it work for your positive benefit by absorbing and assimilating a Scripture verse or even part of a verse. Make up your mind to utilise these four important periods in your day, and with a little determination, you will be able to find others also.

THE DAY THAT BELONGS TO GOD

Finally we consider one other important time in which to meditate – the Lord's Day! One of the first questions people raise when confronted with the importance of Biblical meditation is this: "Whenever will I find time?" The best time to invest in this project is the time that already belongs to God – the Sabbath. God's plan for the Jewish nation was that they accomplished their work in six days so that they would then be able to give God the seventh day in "delighting themselves in the Lord". We Christians need to re-evaluate seriously our Sundays. Some churches need to cut down their activities so that families can have more time at home to meditate and quietly reflect on the goodness of God.

Pascal, the great French philosopher, once said, "Nearly all the ills of life spring from this simple source, that we are not able to sit still in a room." What if our Sabbath were more still? It would be a calming and healing influence in all our lives.

Utilise these important periods in your day.

O God, help me to strike the right balance between work and rest. And protect me from becoming a Christian workaholic. In Jesus' Name. Amen.

THE PURPOSE OF MEDITATION

For Reading and Meditation: Romans 11:33–12:2

"... be transformed by the renewing of your mind ..." (v. 12:2)

At this stage of our studies you may be saying to yourself, "Meditation may be an interesting theory but what is its chief point and purpose?" That is the question we shall try to answer over the next few days. Meditation is designed by God to bring about major changes in our personality, particularly in the realm of our thoughts, feelings and our decisions.

BROUGHT INTO LINE

Since the fall of Adam and Eve in the Garden of Eden, the human personality has been thrown out of line, so to speak, and badly needs readjustment and re-alignment. Consider how that original sin took place. Satan, instead of attempting to put pressure upon Eve's will to reach out and take the forbidden fruit, simply dropped an insinuating doubt into her mind. He knew only too well that God had constructed the personality so that what a human being believes affects the way they feel and how they feel affects the way they act. In other words, our thoughts affect our emotions, and our emotions affect our decisions. Eve, instead of rejecting the doubt which Satan dropped into her mind, allowed it to mingle with her thoughts until soon the doubt led to a dislike of God, and the dislike of God led to disobedience toward God.

Since that day to this, our natural mind is directly contrary to God's principles, and almost every thought we have needs to be brought into line with God's thoughts. This means that we have to train our minds to think as God thinks – and how can we do that? By thinking God's thoughts after Him through continuous and persistent meditation.

We have to train our minds to think as God thinks.

O Father, I see that as I pass on to my emotions and my decisions the result of wrong thinking, I need to saturate my thoughts with Your thoughts, and fill my mind with Your truth. Help me to do this continually and consistently. For Jesus' sake. Amen.

REFOCUSING OUR EMOTIONS

For Reading and Meditation: Psalm 39:1–13

"… and as I meditated,
the fire burned …" (v. 3)

We see from yesterday's reading that in encouraging us to meditate, God has in mind three main purposes: (1) the reconstruction of our thoughts, (2) the refocusing of our emotions and (3) the re-alignment of our wills. Today we consider the second of these purposes – the refocusing of our emotions. Even after we are converted our emotions still continue to manifest "un-Christian" feelings such as anger, bitterness, resentment, jealousy, envy, guilt and many others. We have already observed that our emotions are directly linked to our thoughts so that when we think right, we feel right. If we could think as God thinks then we would feel as God feels.

A RADICAL TRANSFORMATION

There is no doubt in my mind that when we bring our thoughts in line with God's thoughts through Biblical meditation, we are going to experience a radical transformation in our emotions. In a church I pastored 20 years ago, a woman said to me, "My emotions are dulled and deadened. I can feel nothing – joy or sorrow, elation or despair. I have been so hurt that it is impossible for me to respond with feeling to anyone – even God." Life had brought her many difficulties, but I encouraged her to begin meditating. Within three months she had changed beyond recognition. She could laugh, cry, sing and demonstrate emotion in a healthy and positive way. What had happened? The power of God's Word, mingling continually with her thoughts, began to filter through to her emotions and to refocus them so that she was able to enjoy the positive release of her emotions in the way God intended.

When we think right, we feel right.

O Father, if it is true that my thoughts affect my emotions then, from now on, through meditation, I will transmit to them the messages of faith, confidence and power. In Jesus' Name. Amen.

RE-ALIGNMENT OF OUR WILLS

For Reading and Meditation: Hosea 8:1–14

*"I wrote for them the many things of my law,
but they regarded them as something alien." (v. 12)*

We now examine the third main reason why God encourages us to meditate – in order that He may bring about a re-alignment of our wills. The will responds to the feelings and the feelings respond to the thoughts. In other words, we generally choose what makes us feel good, in line with our basic assumptions and thinking. From the moment each one of us enters this world, our will responds to the basic egocentricity within us. We want what we want when we want it. Because of the long years of training at using our will to get what we want, by the time we reach adulthood we are professionals at getting our own way.

At conversion, the will has to be trained to respond to God's directions and purposes, but how can it unless those directions and purposes are stored up in our memory systems through meditation?

FLOODING THE MIND

There are many Christians who consider the Christian life to be simply a battle of the will. They get up every morning, grit their teeth and say to themselves, "I must strive as hard as I can to please God and do everything He wants me to this day." No wonder they fall back into bed at night utterly exhausted and frustrated. Instead of trying to conquer a rebellious will by forcing it to obey God's commands, flood your mind with God's Word by systematic meditation. The more you think God's thoughts, the more your emotions will delight in Him, and the more your emotions delight in Him, the more you will want to obey Him. When the mind is taught to think God's thoughts in meditation, it is not long before the rest of the personality follows the same pattern, and feels and acts in response to right thinking.

The will has to be trained.

Father, I see so clearly that when my will clashes with my thoughts, it produces conflict; when it coincides then it produces concord. Thank You, Father. Amen.

THE MASTER'S VOICE

For Reading and Meditation: Matthew 4:1–11

"… Man does not live on bread alone, but on every word that comes from the mouth of God." (v. 4)

There are three views we can take of our emotions. We can see them as our enemies, as our masters or as our servants. Those who view their emotions as enemies tend to repress them and live out their lives sitting on an unexploded bomb – any moment there can be a big bang. Others view their emotions as their masters, and allow themselves to be pulled and pushed by their negative feelings. The proper way to view our emotions is as our servants – they are there to do our bidding and serve our highest interests.

MADE FOR EACH OTHER

The more we expose our thought life to God's Word in meditation, the more subservient become our emotions. Our personalities were designed by God, and function best when they are indwelt by God. My mind and God's thoughts are not alien – they were made for each other. Jesus said that "Man does not live on bread alone, but on every word that comes from the mouth of God". As the stomach and food are made for each other, we are fashioned in our inner natures for the will of God as expressed in His words. So we "live" on them. We perish on any contradictory word. Notice it says every word. Man's personality thrives when it lives "on every word that comes from the mouth of God"; it perishes when it lives by every word that proceeds out of the mouth of hate, of greed, of fear. When we meditate on God's Word and bring His thoughts into our mind, our emotions recognise their Master's voice, come to attention before Him, and stand alert and ready to do His bidding. Life works in God's way and in no other way. His will is written in His words, and meditating on those words brings peace.

Life works in God's way and in no other way.

O God, help me to fill my mind with Your Word so that my emotions, recognising the Master's voice, can function in the way You designed them to. In Jesus' Name I pray. Amen.

WORKING PRINCIPLES

For Reading and Meditation: Psalm 34:1–8

"I sought the Lord, and he answered me;
he delivered me from all my fears." (v. 4)

In a few days we will begin the task of applying to various areas of our lives the truths we have been discovering over the past few weeks, but before so doing we have one more question to answer: What are the basic working principles of Scripture meditation? There are eight of them in all, the first of which is this: (1) List the various areas of need in your life, as well as questions, decisions or concerns you are presently facing. What are some of the things concerning you at this very moment? Are you depressed? Are you in financial difficulties? Do you need greater patience? Are you troubled by impure thoughts? Put down on a piece of paper a list of the issues that are of major concern to you at this moment.

AN ANSWER FOR EVERYTHING

Once you have done this the next working principle is: (2) Take one thing at a time and find a suitable verse of Scripture that directly relates to the problem. Here you may need help from someone with a greater knowledge of the Bible. Don't hesitate to ask your minister or someone with a good Bible knowledge for this kind of help as it is vitally important to find the right passage of Scripture. If you are depressed it would be quite inappropriate, for example, to meditate on Matthew 1:1–15. Believe me, there is in the Scriptures a particular verse or passage that covers every specific problem you will face. This is why the Bible took so long to be written. God made sure that every conceivable problem had its answer built into His Word before He pronounced it as final and complete.

Take one thing at a time.

Gracious Father, I am thankful for the thought and care that has gone into the compilation of Your Word, the Bible. All the time in designing it You had in mind the solution to all my various needs and problems. I am so grateful. Amen.

For Reading and Meditation: Psalm 104:24–35

"May my meditation be pleasing to him …" (v. 34)

We continue examining the basic working principles of meditation. The next two working principles we must grasp are these: (3) Read the text slowly so that every word sinks in. This present generation is regrettably speed oriented. We "hop" on a bus, "run" down to the shop, "grab" a bite to eat, "race" through the newspaper. Watch the words people use to describe their lifestyle and you will see what I mean. When we come to God's Word we must learn to slow down, stop racing through the Word of God as we would our daily newspaper, and compel our thought processes to ponder every word. (4) Memorise the entire paragraph in which the text appears. It may be that in the past you have had some difficulty in memorising Scripture verses, and if that is so don't be discouraged; at least 95 per cent of the people who begin Scripture memorisation do it convinced that they have poor memories. So you are not alone in this. The truth is that you probably have a perfectly good memory. It simply needs to be developed and trained.

PONDER, REVIEW, REFLECT

The key to memorising is – reviewing. It is not enough simply to remember the word structure of a verse or paragraph – one has to understand its meaning. To do this one needs to review it, reflect upon it, and to do so until its meaning is quite clear. Once the truth of the text is written on the table of the heart then it will not be too difficult to recall it when needed.

We must learn to slow down.

Heavenly Father, help me to learn to apply these principles I have discovered today so that I can really get the best out of Your Word. For Jesus' sake. Amen.

FOCUS ON KEY WORDS

For Reading and Meditation: Psalm 23:1–6

"… he leads me beside quiet waters." (v. 2)

Another working principle of meditation is this: (5) Focus attention on the key words contained in the text. Words reflect feelings and words have sounds – so say them aloud so that your ear can hear them. Emphasise different words within the verse so that you consider it from every point of view. Try this principle on some of your favourite texts. A good one to work with is John 1:12. If you find a verse of Scripture with a word you can't understand then consult a dictionary or a Bible dictionary, or ask someone to help you understand its meaning. It is vitally important that you understand every word in the text. (6) Probe the verse with direct questions. Use the ones newspaper reporters refer to when writing a story: Who? What? Where? When? Why? and How? When you begin to question a verse of Scripture like this, you begin to dissect it and analyse it. Questions are to meditation what food is to living. In some texts, of course, not all these questions will be applicable. Keep in mind that the real purpose of probing the text with questions is to enable your mind to focus on the verse, as this is the exercise which opens the door to the thrilling possibilities in meditation. (7) Visualise exactly what it is you want God to do and see it as done. All great achievements begin with the imagination.

If you are meditating on Psalm 23, then visualise Christ as a Shepherd showing you the way, visualise a quiet, still lake, see in your imagination a beautiful green pasture. The clearer the picture you hold in your mind of what you want God to do for you, the easier it will be for the answer to flow into your personality.

Consider it from every point of view.

O Father, sanctify my imagination so that it becomes an instrument in Your hands to help me visualise Your love, Your power and Your constant caring for my life. In Jesus' Name. Amen.

For Reading and Meditation: Psalm 19:1–14

"May the words of my mouth and the meditation of my heart be pleasing in your sight ..." (v. 14)

The final working principle of meditation is this: (8) Apply the truth of the Scripture to every part of your life immediately you discover it. The crowning glory of meditation is a changed life. Unless meditation brings about changes in your personality then it is an unproductive exercise. This was the problem with the Pharisees. They knew the Word of God and even memorised the Word of God, but they failed to apply it. On one occasion the Lord said to them: "You are of your father the devil" (Jn. 8:44, RSV). Why this stinging rebuke? It was because, with all their knowledge of the Old Testament, there was little change in their attitudes and actions. There was no heart application. They still oppressed the poor, defrauded the widows and became entangled in doubtful business practices.

TRUE FREEDOM

We must be careful about a system of meditation that simply ends in words. True meditation results in positive moral action. So turn your meditation into character development by asking yourself: Is there some truth in this verse which I need to apply in my life at this present moment? Is there something I should stop doing in the light of this verse – a practice, a habit or an activity?

How can I use the truth of this verse to make me more like Jesus Christ? Always bring the fruit of your meditation to the Lord and offer it to Him for His blessing. Ask the Holy Spirit to help you apply God's truth in every part of your personality and enable you to live in conformity to it. It is not enough simply to know the truth – we must allow God to apply it to our lives so that it can set us truly free.

True meditation results in positive moral action.

Father, I see so clearly that the effort I put into Bible meditation is all to no avail unless I can apply it to the areas of my life which need spiritual improvement. Help me to keep this constantly in mind. Amen.

FROM THEORY TO PRACTICE

For Reading and Meditation: I Corinthians 13:1–13

"… But the greatest of these is love." (v. 13)

Having examined over the past month the principles of meditation, it is time now to focus on its practice. Keeping in mind what we learned – that any missing spiritual qualities in our lives can be developed through consistent meditation – we turn now to the task of using the Word of God to enrich our personalities and make us more like Jesus Christ.

NECESSARY QUALITIES

We begin by asking ourselves: What are the qualities on which we must concentrate so as to develop Christlikeness? There are nine of them – all listed for us in Paul's letter to the Galatians chapter 5, verses 22–23: "love, joy, peace, patience, kindness, goodness, faithfulness, gentleness and self-control." John Stott, writing in a pamphlet entitled *Essentials for Tomorrow's Christians* says, "I long to see our evangelical faith exhibiting the fruit of the Spirit. For many years now I have recited to myself every day the ninefold fruit of the Spirit in Gal. 5:22–23 and have prayed for the fullness of the Spirit."

Having the Spirit within, results in a quality of being with nine characteristics. And the first one is love. This emphasis on love being foremost fits in with Paul's emphasis in 1 Corinthians 13. Love is the first outcome of the Spirit within, and if this is lacking, everything is lacking. Make it your goal today to meditate on this priceless passage in 1 Corinthians 13. Do what many Christians do when meditating on verses 4–7 and substitute your name for the word love. How does it sound now? If we want to become more like Jesus then we must grow in love, for without love we are nothing.

Love is the first outcome of the Spirit within.

Father, help me to use Your Word in order primarily to grow in love. Reinforce me there, and then I shall truly grow. In Jesus' Name I pray. Amen.

WITHOUT LOVE – WE ARE NIL

For Reading and Meditation: I Corinthians 8:1–13

"… Knowledge puffs up, but love builds up." (v. 1)

Today we look at another Bible verse which when absorbed into our personality through meditation can assist us in becoming more Christlike in our love. How mature are you as a Christian? You might say, "Well, I have been on the Way a good many years now every way I can." Well, important though knowledge is, it does not, in itself, produce spiritual maturity. J B Phillips translates today's verse thus: "while knowledge may make a man look big, it is only love that can make him grow to his full stature."

LOVE THAT CONTROLS

And this love must not be love in general; it must be love of a specific kind – the love of Christ. Paul, the greatest of all Christians, said, "I am controlled by the love of Christ." This cuts deep into our lives for many are controlled by the love of achievement, love of success or the love of a cause. What kind of love controls you? Is it the love of a cause or the love of Christ? Can you go out into your environment today and bring about changes through the power of Christ's love which dwells in you?

Christ's love flowing in and through our lives is like water. When water moves over an incline and strikes a wheel, it creates power; If it touches a plant, it gives life. Does Christ's love flow into your life in such a measure that it motivates you to creative purposes? Take our verse for today into your mind. Memorise it, probe it, meditate on it and ask yourself: Am I someone who merely has a good deal of knowledge, or am I someone who knows how to love?

It must be love of a specific kind.

Gracious Lord and Master, help me to love as Christ loved, not simply to have an occasional attitude of friendliness and concern, but as something that becomes my whole life. In Jesus' Name. Amen.

REJOICE AT ALL TIMES

For Reading and Meditation: I Thessalonians 5:12–24

"... rejoice at all times ..." (v. 16, Moffatt)

We turn now to the second fruit of the Spirit – joy. It is no accident that joy follows love, for joy is a by-product of love. Are you a joyful Christian? Do non-Christians see in you an exuberance that is not of this world? Joy should be the central characteristic of every Christian, and yet a lot of Christians know little or nothing of it. They are under the lash of duty rather than under the control of an inner delight. Some not only don't expect joy – they don't want it. Life has to be lived seriously, but faith with an Easter morning in it must express itself in abounding joy. Joy, not gloom, is our spiritual birthright. We are made for joy, and if there is gloom then there is something wrong. The empty tomb takes away our empty gloom. To a Christian, joy is inevitable.

The text we have chosen for meditation purposes today is brief but powerful: "rejoice at all times ..." Note – at all times. This is where it becomes necessary to probe the text and ask ourselves: Does it really mean "at all times"? Perhaps it means sometimes, most times or during good times. Think for a moment. To thank God for everything means we must see God in everything. When we face times of gloom and sadness, the thing to do is to look trouble in the eye and say: "If God has allowed you to come then it can only be to help me and not to hurt me. So I will do what the psalmist did – make a joyful noise to the rock of my salvation." If you do then, believe me, from that rock you will get a joyful echo in return.

We must see God in everything.

Lord, in a world that is so full of gloom and sadness, help me to share Your deep, eternal joy with everyone I meet today. In Jesus' Name I pray.

For Reading and Meditation: John 15:5–17

"… that my joy may be in you and that your joy may be complete." (v. 11)

This important passage shows us that we cannot absorb Christ's joy into our lives without it affecting our own joy. Listen to the text in Moffatt's translation: "I have told you this, that my joy may be within you and your joy complete." You cannot take His joy without finding your own joy complete. His joy completes our joy. The idea that Christian joy is a projected joy that we will one day discover in heaven, instead of an intrinsic joy that supports us while we are on earth, is false. Some Christians creak in soul and body joints as they make their way to glory. They may be making for glory but they don't appear to be walking the glory road now.

OVERFLOWING JOY

Look at what the Bible says in this little cameo of Scripture verses concerning joy: "let us enjoy the peace we have with God" (Rom. 5:1, Moffatt). Some have peace with God but don't enjoy it. Here's another passage: "we enjoy our redemption" (Eph. 1:7, Moffatt). To be redeemed and not enjoy it, is a contradiction in terms. Again: "we both enjoy our access to the Father in one Spirit" (Eph. 2:18, Moffatt). And finally: "we enjoy our confidence of free access" (Eph. 3:12, Moffatt). In these passages joy is overflowing because of peace, redemption and access to the Father. I guarantee that, however dark and dismal your surroundings, if you will meditate on the fact that God is your Father, Jesus is your Saviour, the angels are your companions, heaven is your home, and you have free access to the throne of God then joy will spring up in you because it must. To a Christian, joy is more than a luxury – it is a necessity.

Joy will spring up in you because it must.

O Father, I am so grateful to You for showing me that my joy can only be full when I link myself to Christ's joy. As I link myself to You in meditation so You will link Yourself to me in deep, abiding joy. I am so grateful. Amen.

PERFECT PEACE

For Reading and Meditation: John 14:15–27

*"Peace I leave with you; my peace
I give you …" (v. 27)*

We come now to the third spiritual quality we must possess if we are to be Christlike in character – the quality of peace. Before we go into the matter of spiritual peace, let's get one thing straight – we are talking here about more than peace of mind, we are talking about peace of spirit. There are many who turn to religion to give them peace of mind. A woman told me once, "I turned to religion [religion, mark you, not Christ] to obtain peace of mind and although it helped me greatly, it couldn't compare with the experience I discovered in Transcendental Meditation." This lady was looking for peace of mind, and the very term she used showed the shallowness of her quest.

THE GOD OF PEACE

You cannot have peace of mind unless you have something deeper than peace of mind. Peace – the peace of God – begins not in the mind but in the spirit. When we have peace at the depths of our spirit then peace of mind is the outcome of that deeper peace. You cannot truly have peace of mind if there is a conflict in the spirit. One able preacher puts it like this: "In order to know the peace of God, you must first know the God of peace." You see, to tinker with the mind and leave the depths untouched is unproductive; it simply produces a peace that goes to pieces.

True peace comes from adjustment to reality, and there can be no adjustment to reality without adjustment to God. Peace of mind breaks down if the worm of doubt is eating at its centre. When calamity comes it breaks apart. Christian peace flows out of a right personal relationship with God and His Son the Lord Jesus Christ.

The peace of God begins in the spirit.

Gracious Father, I know that it is only in You that I can find perfect peace. Touch me at the depths of my spirit, and help me to open myself to Your perfect peace. In Jesus' Name. Amen.

"THINGS FALL APART"

For Reading and Meditation: Isaiah 26:1–12

"You will keep in perfect peace him whose mind is steadfast, because he trusts in you." (v. 3)

Although true peace begins in a right relationship with God, this verse shows us that in order for it to continue there must be a conscious centring of the mind on God. The Almighty must not be the place of occasional reference; He must be the centre of our affections and our loyalty. And, more than that, He must be the centre of our trust – "because he trusts in you". W B Yeats in describing what happens to those who do not trust in God, put it thus:

> *Things fall apart; the centre cannot hold.*
> *Mere anarchy is loosed upon the world …*
> *The best lack all conviction, while the worst*
> *Are full of passionate intensity.*

"Things fall apart; the centre cannot hold" for the simple reason that the centre is not "stayed" on God. People thought that the accumulation of material things would stave off anxiety, only to discover that it increased it.

"GADGETITIS"

A man told me once that his wife had caught the disease called "gadgetitis". I had never before heard of it so I asked him to describe the symptoms. He said, "Well, when she gets a gadget she becomes unhappy because she wonders how long it will be before they bring out another gadget that will make this one obsolete. Then she worries whether or not she will be able to afford it when it comes out." If we are to enjoy perfect peace then God, and God alone, must become the centre of our affections. Draw out of this verse all that God has put into it, this very day: "You will keep in perfect peace him whose mind is steadfast."

He must be the centre of our affections.

Father, thank You, for showing me that my security is not to be found in earth's securities, but comes from being secure in You. Help me to fix the focus of my life entirely on You. In Jesus' Name. Amen.

PLAYING GOD'S TAPES

For Reading and Meditation: Philippians 4:1–9

"... whatever is true ... noble ... right ... pure ...
lovely ... admirable ... think about such things." (v. 8)

We saw earlier in our studies that what we think about or meditate upon greatly affects the way we feel. Here before us today is the classic passage on this discipline. Among the things Paul bids us to think upon not one is negative. If you constantly think on the untrue, the dishonest, the unjust, the impure, the ugly, the things of evil report and the things that are unpraiseworthy then the very disharmony of those things will invade your whole personality and destroy you. But, if on the other hand, you do what the great apostle suggests then what is the result? This: "the God of peace shall be with you" (v. 9).

NEW TAPES FOR OLD

Earlier this morning, before writing this page, I woke up with a start. I don't know whether it was a dream that startled me or a sudden sound, but my heart was beating wildly. For a moment I was panic-stricken, but then I began to put this principle into operation. I said to myself, "God is with me and guards me every moment of my life. He will allow nothing to happen to me unless it is for my good. So whatever is happening, I know God is in control." In minutes I was asleep again.

Inside us is a kind of tape recorder which repeatedly plays back the negative things we have heard and believed since childhood. It is the playing of these tapes that often causes us so much anxiety. God has given us in the Bible some new tapes which when played and listened to bring about great changes in every part of our personality. So throw away the old tapes, and begin to listen to the things God has to say about your life. He loves you, guards you, provides for you, and is in control of your entire destiny.

Listen to the things God has to say about your life.

O Father, help me to get rid of the negative tapes which when played destroy my personality. Help me instead to listen to Your tapes by meditating on Your Word. In Jesus' Name. Amen

GOOD TEMPER

For Reading and Meditation: Hebrews 12:1–11

"… let us lay aside every weight … and let us run with patience the race that is set before us." (v. 1, AV)

The next spiritual quality we shall examine is patience. Moffatt translates this word as "good temper" (Gal. 5:22) while the AV calls it "long-suffering". Someone has suggested that long-suffering is love stretched out; it is so elastic and tough that it doesn't break apart into bad temper. It maintains good temper amidst the pressures and difficulties of human events. Some people believe that Jesus lost His temper in the synagogue at Capernaum where it says: "And he looked around at them with anger" (Mk. 3:5, RSV). Also when He stung the souls of the Pharisees with the words: "Woe unto you ... hypocrites!" (Matt. 23:13–15).

CONSTRUCTIVE ANGER

Was Jesus really displaying signs of bad temper? No of course not. He was "grieved at their hardness of heart". This added phrase lights up the situation with regard to His looking at them with anger. The anger Jesus felt was grief – grief at their insensitivity to human need. It was grief at what was happening to someone with a distressing physical affliction not personal pique at what was happening to Him. That made His anger constructive and not destructive. Let's face it, more often that not our anger is really bad temper.

Our ego becomes wounded and we lash back in retaliation. Good temper is redemptive temper. It burns with the steady fire of redemptive intention; retaliative temper just burns you up. Notice I say. "burns *you* up". It was intended to burn the other fellow, but all it succeeds in doing is burn you. Good temper, however, has a redemptive intention in all its attitudes and acts.

Good temper is redemptive temper.

Father, help me, from this day forward, to direct my temper towards redemptive ends so that the purposes of Your Kingdom are realised. For Jesus' sake I ask it. Amen.

"HONK AWAY – IT'S YOUR ULCER"

For Reading and Meditation: I Corinthians 13:1–13

*"Love is patient, love is kind. It does not envy ...
It is not rude ... it is not easily angered ..." (vv. 4–5)*

Temper can be either good or bad according to the intention behind it. Someone has said that there are two ways to blow your car horn – the Christian way and the un-Christian way. The Christian way very gently calls attention to a situation; the un-Christian way not only calls attention to a situation, but it also calls attention to what the honker feels about the situation. I saw a sign on the back of an American car in New York that said: "Honk away – it's your ulcer." Although ulcers have a number of different causes, many of them are the visible signs of an ulcerated spirit – ulcerated by fears, resentments and guilts.

YOUR TEMPER WILL FIND YOU OUT

A book I looked at today, while doing a little research on the subject of temper, referred to a Western convert to Hinduism who was lecturing on the poise and peace of Hindu mysticism. Suddenly, while gesticulating, he accidentally struck the lamp on the table, sending it crashing to the ground. He immediately lost his temper and, of course, lost his audience at the same time!

The same book told the story of a non-Christian psychiatrist interviewing a man who was full of conflicts. In the middle of the interview the 'phone rang, and because of a mistake in the number, the psychiatrist swore at his secretary. He lost his patience and his patient, for the patient saw that he had little to give except verbal advice. When we lose our tempers and our patience, and take it out on those around us, we do something to ourselves. We give people a piece of our mind and lose our own peace of mind. Focus on the verse before you today, and ask God to give you the temper that remains unperturbed during provocation, and sweet amid surrounding bitterness.

The temper that remains unperturbed.

Yes, Father, grant that I may be the peaceful exception amid disturbed surroundings, at rest amid restlessness. For Jesus' sake. Amen.

WRONG MEANS – WRONG ENDS

For Reading and Meditation: James 1:19–27

"… for man's anger does not bring about the righteous life that God desires." (v. 20)

Some Christians feel that they have to show impatience and bad temper in order to get things done. A minister said to me, "But if I don't lose my temper occasionally and threaten the people, they will never do anything for the Lord." But the verse before us makes it quite plain. Listen to it in the J B Phillips' translation: "For man's temper is never the means of achieving God's true goodness." It is the case of wrong means trying to get to right ends. Wrong means get to wrong ends – inevitably.

A BASIC DECISION

Many years ago I received a stinging rebuke from someone who set out to criticise me. My first reaction was to write off a bitter retaliation. But, after prayer, I was able to resist the temptation, and instead I wrote a polite reply. Back came another equally critical letter. This time I decided I would give the man concerned a taste of his own medicine. But again, after prayer, I resisted and wrote a polite note of acceptance. You can imagine my reaction when a few days later I received a third letter from the man, and my first impulse was to throw the letter away and not even read it. I opened it, however, and a cheque for £100 for the work of the Crusade for World Revival dropped out. In his letter he apologised for his wrong spirit and said, "God showed me through your gentle reaction to my bitter letters that I was moving in a wrong direction. Now I have surrendered my life to Him and dedicated my all to His service." So make up your mind to fix it as one of life's basic decisions – no bad temper ever, good temper always.

Wrong means get to wrong ends.

O Father, help me to meet all impatience with patience, all hate with love, all grumpiness with joy. In Jesus' Name. Amen.

"THE HIGH WATER MARK"

For Reading and Meditation: Philippians 2:1–11

*"Your attitude should be the same as that
of Christ Jesus." (v. 5)*

We come now to the next fruit of the Spirit – kindness. Someone has said, "Without kindness there is no virtue in the other virtues. Love, joy, peace, good temper without kindness are incomplete. So it is not chance that the middle virtue of the nine is kindness; it puts the flavour into all the others." Indeed the spirit of kindness pervades everything. In the Old Testament we often read the word "lovingkindness". A little boy when asked to describe the difference between kindness and lovingkindness said, "Kindness is when your mother gives you a piece of bread and butter; lovingkindness is when she puts jam on it as well!"

AN INFINITE PLUS

In the New Testament, however, a content has gone into the word kindness which makes the addition of the word loving unnecessary. The verse before us today illustrates that: "Treat one another with the same spirit as you experience in Christ Jesus" (Moffatt). Notice it emphasises not just the actions but the spirit that underlies the actions. This means that we are not only to follow the same actions of Jesus but the same spirit that prompted those actions. A Bible commentator says of this verse, "This is the high-water mark of morality in the universe. Beyond this the human race will not, and cannot, progress. This is a character and a conduct ultimate. This gives kindness a plus – an infinite plus." As Christians we are called to be as kind as Jesus would be if He were in our shoes in any particular situation. With this redemptive content put into kindness, we must make it our goal to carry the Spirit of Jesus with us every-where we go.

*This is the
high-water
mark of
morality.*

O Father, help me to cover all ugly unkindness with the same robe of kindness with which You cover it. And keep me from the unkind silence as well as the unkind word. In Jesus' Name. Amen.

"UNUSUAL KINDNESS"

For Reading and Meditation: Matthew 25:31–46

"… whatever you did for one of the least of these brothers of mine, you did for me." (v. 40)

The importance of kindness can be seen when we consider how long an act of kindness shown to us stays in our memory when other events are quickly forgotten. The people of Madras, India, have treated me with many honours – large crowds, eager listeners and responsive congregations. but the one thing that stands out in my memory is the act of an unknown lady who one night pushed through the crowd of people around me and handed me a small flower. I knew it was all she had, and she wanted to show her gratitude in this small but meaningful way for the blessing God had brought. That flower is as fresh in my memory as the day on which I received it.

NEVER TO BE FORGOTTEN

But just as an act of kindness sticks in the memory so does an act of unkindness also remain. A writer tells of going down a lane with a nursemaid when two village children ran out and offered him some wild flowers. He remembers how he haughtily rejected the flowers, and ran back and took the hand of his nursemaid. When he looked back and saw the two children standing and looking at him with tears running down their faces, he was deeply upset. His comment on that moment was this: "There I first authentically rejected the Kingdom of God."

If both acts of kindness and acts of unkindness stick in people's memories, let's make up our minds that from now on with God's help, we will seek to be kinder than we have ever been before. Paul in looking back at the experience of his shipwreck on the island of Malta remembered one thing particularly. He said, "The islanders showed us unusual kindness" (Acts 28:2).

Let's make up our minds to be kinder than ever before.

O Father, help me to be alert to those today who need my kindness, and help me to give it graciously and generously. In Jesus' Name I pray. Amen.

"THAT WAS GREAT MEDICINE"

For Reading and Meditation: Romans 12:9–21

*"Be kindly ... one to another with
brotherly love ..." (v. 10, AV)*

Kindness is not a luxury; it is a moral, spiritual and physical "must". Kindness by its very nature is an outgoing attitude. Whenever it is present in someone's life it breaks the stranglehold of self-preoccupation, and gives instead an attitude of other-interest. And other-interest is good for us spiritually, psychologically and physically.

A SPIRITUAL SICKNESS

A doctor wrote out a prescription for a sick man which went like this: "Go down to the bus station in the centre of town and find someone who needs you then do something for them." The man thought the doctor was joking, but the physician said, "Unless you do this I will not be able to help you further." He went down to the bus station, and after standing around for the best part of an hour, he spotted a woman sitting on her suitcase in great distress. Upon asking her what was wrong, he discovered that her daughter was to have met her but hadn't, and she had no idea of her address or telephone number. The man set about trying to find her address from the telephone directory, and after 'phoning different numbers, he eventually tracked down the woman's daughter. His next step was to hire a taxi and take her to her daughter's house. On the way he bought her some flowers, and finally delivered her to the daughter amid the tearful gratitude of both. The following day he visited his doctor and said, "Doctor, that was great medicine. I feel better already." Kindness is a "must". If you are unkind to anyone, you are a sick person or on the road to being sick. Unkindness is a spiritual sickness which will possibly issue in physical sickness.

*Kindness
is a must.*

O Father, help me to overlook no opportunity this day of being kind to everybody in every situation. In Jesus' Name. Amen.

GENEROSITY GENERATES

For Reading and Meditation: Matthew 6:19–24

" … if your Eye is generous, the whole of your body will be illumined." (v. 22, Moffatt)

The next fruit of the Spirit is generosity. Some translations and paraphrases prefer the word goodness here, but I feel J B Phillips and others capture the real meaning of the original word when they translate it as generosity.

FULL OF LIGHT

The verse I have selected for today's meditation shows us that when our eye – our outlook on life, our whole way of looking at things and people – is generous then our personality becomes illuminated and lit up from within. Jesus was generous towards everyone and, therefore, His whole personality was full of light. When we come in contact with Jesus Christ, and allow His Spirit to permeate and pervade our lives then that same generosity is generated within us. The generous eye and the generous attitude are the basis of all sound human relationships.

When Ananias, a potential victim of Saul's hostility and rage, was told by the Lord that Saul needed his help, he went immediately to where Saul was, put his hand upon him and said, "Brother Saul." Brother Saul? – this was the very man who had come to murder him and his fellow Christians. But generosity in the heart of Ananias opened the gates of life to a broken man, and started the greatest Christian of the centuries on his way. I firmly believe that the generous and forgiving attitude of Ananias at that moment was one of the means in God's hand that produced the change in the heart of Saul. As you fix today's verse firmly in your mind, and begin to meditate upon it, ask the Lord to help you this day and every day to lay generosity at the basis of all your dealings with everybody, everywhere.

Our personality becomes illuminated.

Yes, heavenly Father, help me to be the channel and not the stopping place of all Your generosity to me. In Jesus' Name I pray. Amen.

THE SECOND MILE

For Reading and Meditation: Matthew 5:38–48

*"If anybody forces you to go a mile with him, do more
– go two miles with him." (v. 41, J B Phillips)*

Someone has pointed out that in the list of the nine
qualities of the fruit of the Spirit, six of them are
attitudes we should have toward others – love, good temper,
kindness, generosity, fidelity and gentleness – the other three
are attitudes we should have toward ourselves – joy, peace
and self-control. Does this mean that we should have twice
as much interest in our relationships with others than we
have in our relationship with ourselves? It would seem so.
The more we surrender to the Holy Spirit, allowing Him to
have control over us, the greater will be our interest in
others and the lesser the interest in ourselves. It is what one
writer calls "the second mile attitude in human virtues".

THE UNBREAKABLE TIE

We said yesterday that the generous eye and the generous
attitude are the basis of all sound relationships. The Nor-
wegians and the Swedes have a closeness and a brotherliness
that has always impressed me. Although they are quite
different from each other, there seems to be an unbreakable
tie that binds them as one. When I remarked on this some
years ago during a visit to the two countries, I was told the
reason for this unbreakable tie. When Norway was joined to
Sweden many years ago, there came a time when Norway
wanted her freedom. Without any arguments or long-
drawn-out discussions, Sweden gave it out of the Christian
spirit that operated within the ruling family of Sweden at
that time. The generosity, in giving freedom without war or
bitterness, has resulted in a basic soundness that is evident in
their present relationships. The generous eye filled with light
the whole body of human relationships between the people
of two different countries.

The basis of all sound rela-tionships.

O Father, I see so clearly that so often the first mile doesn't
register; it's the second mile that counts. With Your help I'm
going to be a second miler. Amen.

SUPPOSE – JUST SUPPOSE

For Reading and Meditation: 2 Corinthians 8:1–15

"… see that you also excel in this grace of giving." (v. 7)

We continue examining the importance of building into our lives, through the grace and strength of Jesus Christ, the quality of generosity. How generous are we with our finances, for example? Remember, what happens to your money happens to you. Your money is an extended or contracted you. If you pile up your money with no purpose behind it, it will clog your soul; you will become a purposeless self, hence an unhappy self.

FAMOUS FOR GIVING

Suppose when Jesus wanted to feed the hungry five thousand and blessed the loaves before distributing them, the disciples had said to themselves: "Let's not serve them out, let's save them up – we will keep them in a corner and make the multitude pay for them." What would have happened? The connection between earth and heaven would have been broken, the supply would have stopped, and we would never have heard of those disciples again.

Suppose the man who owned the colt, when the disciples told him the Lord needed his colt, had replied, "I also have need of him." What would have happened? For the rest of his life that man would have had an inner conflict over the question of the colt, and would have spent his days trying to justify the unjustifiable. But after he gladly let Jesus have it, the colt came back to him – the most famous colt in history.

Suppose again the little boy had refused to let Jesus have his five loaves and two fish, insisting they were his. What would have happened? There would have been no miracle, and an important section of the New Testament would be missing. The little boy who was generous, although unnamed, became one of the most famous boys of history.

What happens to your money happens to you.

Gracious Father, as You have opened to me the door of Your heart, help me to open up the door of my heart to others. In Jesus' Name I pray. Amen.

For Reading and Meditation: Matthew 25:14–30

"... You have been faithful with a few things;
I will put you in charge of many things ..." (v. 21)

We come now to the next fruit of the Spirit – fidelity. One writer says he is surprised that Paul did not place this quality at the head of the list and make it first. One well known organisation, famous for its four absolutes, does precisely this – absolute honesty, absolute purity, absolute unselfishness and absolute love. Paul, however, instead of putting honesty and fidelity first and love last, puts love first and fidelity towards the end of the list. Is he right? Yes, for the primary basis of the Christian faith is love. The first and second great commandments begin, "Thou shalt love ..." (Luke 10:27).

THE FRUIT OF SURRENDER

If the primary thing in Christianity is honesty then this roots our religion in the will. If the primary thing is love then this roots it in the emotions. If the centre of our faith is in an act of the will then religion means a whipping up of the will and determined self-effort. But if the centre of our religion is not in the will but in the emotions, and we surrender the will to the object of the emotions – God – then religion is not a straining to be good, but a love affair with the Creator of the universe. So Paul puts honesty and fidelity as a fruit of our surrender to Jesus Christ and the Holy Spirit. Jesus once said, "He who is faithful with a trifle is also faithful with a large trust, and he who is dishonest with a trifle is also dishonest with a large trust" (Luke 16:10, Moffatt). Here the basic principle is laid down. If you are not honest with a trifle, you can't be trusted with the tremendous. God tests us with a little before He entrusts to us a lot.

A love affair with the Creator of the universe.

Father, I see so clearly that every day You are testing me with a little. Help me to be faithful there then I shall be faithful in the greater and bigger things. Amen.

"TRUTH IN THE INWARD PARTS"

For Reading and Meditation: Psalm 51:1–12

*"... thou desirest truth in the
inward parts ..." (v. 6, AV)*

We continue examining the quality of honesty and fidelity. Both the universe and ourselves are made for truth and honesty, and both the universe and ourselves are alien to untruth and dishonesty. In other words, the universe is made for the same thing we are made for – righteousness. The world in which we live is not made for the success of a lie; a lie breaks itself upon the moral universe, perhaps not today, nor even tomorrow, but one day – most certainly.

SAND OR OIL?

The Tamils of South India have a saying, "The life of the cleverest lie is only eight days." The Germans used to say, "Lies have short legs." Good in the short run but bad in the long run! During the Second World War some of the people changed it to, "Lies have one short leg," for Goebbels, the propagandist minister, had one short leg. A great philosopher once said, "The ultimate question about a man's character is this: Will that man lie? Are there any circumstances under which he will lie? If so, the rest of his character is worthless – basically he is unsound."

I knew a Christian worker who would work himself to the bone for the church. He was ready to step out of his home at any hour of the day or night in order to bring help to someone. But he could never overcome his proneness to lie. That basic falsity cancelled out almost all the rest. Gradually he began to lose his self-respect, and although he tried hard to continue his good works, he lost interest – in himself and in others. The moral universe had the last word. Dishonesty puts sand in the machinery of life; honesty and fidelity put oil. We can choose to live with either sand or oil in the machinery of our soul.

*A lie
breaks
itself
upon the
moral
universe.*

Father, I am so grateful that You made me for truth in my inner parts. Help me not to violate the rule of my being. In Jesus' Name I pray. Amen.

SATAN'S FIRST LIE

For Reading and Meditation: Romans 13:1–14

"Let us walk honestly ..." (v. 13, AV)

One of the questions I am often asked is this: Is a lie ever justifiable? My answer is a categorical "No". The issue (so I believe) can be settled forever by the fact that God cannot lie (Num. 23:19). And He cannot delegate to you or me the privilege of lying for Him. The New Testament is quite adamant on the matter: "Lie not one to another" (Col. 3:9). In fact the last book of the Bible makes it quite clear that "all liars, shall have their part in the lake which burneth with fire and brimstone" (Rev. 21:8). Strong words! But they are God's words.

A LITTLE MORE

We must fix it firmly in our minds that no one gets away with anything in a moral universe if that "anything" is dishonest. God's Word to Adam was this, "... when you eat of it you will surely die" (Gen. 2:17). But Satan countered this with the very first lie: "You will not surely die" (Gen. 3:4). He keeps repeating this well-worn but utterly discredited lie to every son of Adam, but when we are dishonest and untruthful then something dies within us. Death eats away at our heart the moment dishonesty comes in. When I asked a minister the other day what he thought was the quality most needed by the members of his church, he said, "Fidelity." He added, "Many sing, 'Take my life and let it be ...' yet five minutes after the service, they forget their song of dedication and are at each other's throats." I hope it isn't as bad as that in your church, but I suspect all who are reading these lines today will confess that under the searching light of God's divine X-ray, we could all do with a little more fidelity. Let's decide, through meditation on God's Word, to bring a little more of it into our lives each day.

> *When we are dishonest and untruthful, something dies within us.*

Father, I see that no dishonesty is worth the price I have to pay for it – inward conflict and unhappiness. Help me to be a person of honesty and fidelity. In Jesus' Name. Amen.

For Reading and Meditation: I Peter 5:1–11

"... clothe yourselves with humility ..." (v. 5)

We come now to the eighth fruit of the Spirit – gentleness or as the Good News Bible puts it – humility. As we grow in the spiritual life, one of the greatest dangers we have to face is pride. Many fall because of it. I have seen young men start out in the ministry with tremendous potential, but they became proud and self-opinionated with the result that they lost their spiritual power and effectiveness.

OUR REAL HEIGHT

I read one morning a report of a writer who said, "Yesterday I went out after a storm and found a beautiful branch from a tree broken off and lying in the pathway. Parasites had done it. Great bunches of a parasite had weakened it, and when the test of the storm came it broke and fell." The most dangerous parasite is spiritual pride – many are weakened by it and fall in the time of testing. This is why we must begin to meditate on the Bible texts that remind us of the importance of humility so that we can, through assimilating the Word of God into our spirits, begin to take on the characteristic of true humility. What is humility? Philip Brooks says, "The true way to be humble is not to stoop until you are smaller than yourself but to stand at your real height against some higher nature that will show you what the real smallness of your greatness is." Can you see what he is saying? Humility is not grovelling in the dust saying, "I am a worm," but standing at your very highest, looking at Christ and being forever humble. When we lose sight of Christ then self looms large.

The most dangerous parasite is spiritual pride.

O Father, help me to fill my mind with thoughts of Your greatness so that I shall always see the real smallness of my greatest greatness. In Jesus' Name. Amen.

For Reading and Meditation: Colossians 2:16–23

"Such regulations indeed have an appearance of
wisdom, with their ... false humility ..." (v. 23)

We said yesterday that "the true way to be humble is not to stoop until you are smaller than yourself but to stand at your real height against some higher nature that will show you what the real smallness of your greatest greatness is". A Hindu teacher of transcendental meditation who arrived recently at London Airport, was quoted as saying, "I used to believe at one time in idols but now I believe that I myself am God." He gave up his idols and made one of himself.

GREAT IN GOD

Whenever we lose sight of the true God, we lose the source of our humility. I love to ponder that matchless passage in John 13 which says, "Jesus, knowing that the Father had given all things into his hands, and that he had come from God and was going to God ... girded himself with a towel ... and began to wash the disciples feet" (vv. 3–5, RSV). The secret of Jesus' humility on that occasion was the consciousness of His greatness: "Knowing ... that he had come from God and was going to God ..." The small dare not be humble. With a wrong view of themselves, they constantly try to add to their stature by every means at their disposal. The Church needs to be rid of a false view of humility (i.e. those with a low opinion of themselves) which circulates amongst its members and which takes the position that they ought to be constantly denigrating and downgrading themselves. That is not humility; that is inferiority. When, following conversion, we see ourselves as we really are – as being great in God – then from that sense of greatness flows a true humility. Being in God makes us great – and humble. Great because humble and humble because great.

The small dare not be humble.

O Father, help me never to lose sight of Christ for He alone is the reference point against which I can measure my humility. Amen.

For Reading and Meditation: Colossians 3:1–14

"Therefore, as God's chosen people ... clothe yourselves with compassion, kindness, humility ..." (v. 12)

As so many Christians are confused over the difference between inferiority and humility, we shall spend another day in examining this question. A Christian leader tells of a woman who worked in his organisation, and who one day approached him thus: "Bruce, aren't you glad that we are nothing and the Lord is everything." When he hesitated to agree with the first part of her statement, she added, "I just wish more people would realise they are nothing, then God could really be exalted."

TRUE WORTH

Many Christians, like that dear woman, fail to see the difference between humility and inferiority. To these people humility is downgrading oneself, undervaluing one's abilities, considering oneself less capable than others and thinking in terms of perpetual self-abasement. People who hold this view of humility often quote Philippians 2:3 in support of their argument, but let's examine the passage one more time. Here, according to Paul, Christ is our example of humility. Jesus most certainly did not see Himself as inferior or worthless in the sight of others. He knew His worth, and since He had a secure identity, He did not have to flaunt His strengths. He was free to put aside His own interests for the benefit of others. Humility hinges on this important point – by adopting a proper attitude toward ourselves. Once you see yourself in Christ, and learn to recognise your true worth and value to Him and others, you are free to put aside your own interests for the sake of others. When we reach out to others from this position of inner strength we can then, and only then, manifest true humility.

Christ is our example of humility.

Father, help me to understand this most important point so that never again will I confuse inferiority with humility. This I ask in Christ's peerless and precious Name. Amen.

SELF-CONTROL

For Reading and Meditation: 2 Corinthians 5:11–21

"For the love of Christ constrains us ..." (v. 14, NKJV)

We come now to the last of the nine qualities of the fruit of the Spirit – self-control. It is interesting to note that Paul puts self-control last. Most systems of thought would put it first. Confucius believed that self-control would produce the "superior man". Hinduism believes that self-control will produce the "realised man". Stoicism believes that self-control will produce the "detached man". Transcendental meditation believes that self-control will produce the "happy man". The Christian approach is different. It emphasises love for Christ as being the first priority, and self-control as the last. In other words you do not gain love through self-control, but you gain self-control through love.

RELAXED AND RELEASED

In the verse that we have selected for our meditation today, Paul says, "The love of Christ constrains us," or literally "narrow us to His way" – controls us. You see, if you begin with self-control then *you* are the centre, *you* are controlling yourself. And you will become anxious and apprehensive lest you slip out from beneath your control. But if you begin, as Paul does here, with love then the motivation of your life is love for a person, someone outside of yourself – Jesus. You are then released from yourself and from self-preoccupation. This makes you a relaxed and a released person. When you begin with love, you end with self-control; when you begin with self-control, you end up not with love but with anxiety, nervousness and apprehension. The whole emphasis of the New Testament is on controlling ourselves by the force and power of our love for Christ. "Love Christ and do what you like" for you'll like what He likes.

You are then released from yourself.

Father, from today onward my self-control shall be rooted in Christ-control, and then it will no longer be insecure and precarious. Amen.

For Reading and Meditation: Philippians 4:10–20

"I can do everything through him who gives me strength." (v. 13)

W e ended yesterday with that famous statement of Pascal's – "Love Christ and do what you like." When we love Christ we will like what He likes. In a church where I preached recently I heard a man testify to the fact that before his conversion he had been an alcoholic. He said that he had spent ten years of his life trying to get control of himself, but one night he got down on his knees and let Christ control him, and he never touched a drop of alcohol again. He found self-control through Christ-control.

ONE SUPREME CONTROL

For a time in my teens I tried to live the Christian life from the standpoint of self-control. Every day I would start out with the determination to control my habits and avoid my favourite sins. And every night I dropped back into bed feeling an utter failure. How could an uncontrolled will control an uncontrolled self? A diseased will could not heal a diseased soul, and so I resigned myself to continuing my old life of sinful habits and pleasures. Then one night the Holy Spirit came to me and showed me the reality of the situation. I was trying to live the Christian life in my own strength. I surrendered to Christ and at once He took over my affections. I began to love Him, and within days the lesser loves began to drop away. I saw that I had been trying to control the margin of my life while something else had been controlling the centre – self. Christ came in and took over the central control – the control of self – then together He and I dealt with the marginal problems. Have one supreme control – the love of Christ – and all other loves will fit into their proper place.

Self-control through Christ-control.

Lord Jesus, help me to tolerate no competing loves within me. Help me to make You supreme Ruler and Lord. For Your own dear Name's sake. Amen.

For Reading and Meditation: Galatians 2:14–20

"I have been crucified with Christ and I no longer live, but Christ lives in me." (v. 20)

We are seeing that self-control for a Christian is the result of Christ-control – Christ living in the personality by the power of the Holy Spirit. We begin our lives in this world with a high degree of self-indulgence. Our nature, being basically self-centred and egocentric, wants to have its own way and revels in the things that bring pleasure to our personalities, irrespective of whether these things are forbidden by God or not. Self-indulgence, however, leads to self-exhaustion. It is not long before fears, resentments, inhibitions, guilts, flood into the personality. Then begins the vicious cycle of trying to overcome the self-defeating nature of sin by a host of sinful pleasures and devices.

A NEW DYNAMIC

Some people never get past this point but go down into the grave unconverted and unfulfilled. Those who become Christians, however, pass from the point of self-indulgence and self-exhaustion to self-surrender. As they give themselves to Jesus Christ, He comes in, takes over the control of the centre, provides the personality with a new dynamic and new thrust, enabling the person to move toward the next stage of development – self-control. And self-control leads ultimately to self-realisation, for only those who have themselves under control can know self-realisation. A doctor I know who helped others break the smoking habit, was unsuccessful in his own attempts to give up smoking. He received Christ and stopped smoking – suddenly and decisively. He said, "I felt like a man walking out of prison. I was free." Through Christ he found a mastery that was not in his own nature, giving him a self-control which led to self-realisation.

Self-control leads ultimately to self-realisation.

Father, I've tried the way of self-indulgence which leads only to self-exhaustion. Help me always to take the way of self-surrender, for it is only this that leads to self-control and self-realisation. Amen.

THE DEVIL'S SPARK

For Reading and Meditation: Proverbs 23:6–26

"For as he thinketh in his heart,
so is he ..." (v. 7, AV)

On this last day of our studies on the subject of Getting the best out of the Bible, it is now time to summarise what we have been saying over these past seven weeks. We have seen that to read, study, memorise and even analyse the Bible is not enough – to get the best out of it, we must spend time meditating upon it. If we are to grow in Christlikeness then we must learn that what we hold in our minds passes automatically into our emotions and from there affects our decisions and ultimately our actions.

HARNESSING THE POWER

Thoughts are powerful – they are not passive things. If, for example, we dally with sex thoughts, and allow our imagination to dwell upon things that are impure and forbidden by God then it will not be long before the dallying turns into doing. A Dr George A Buttrick says, "We dramatise temptation in our secret thoughts thus gathering gasoline for the devil's spark. And then we wonder why we blow up!" What we take into our minds in meditation will stay in our lives as fact. Our secret meditations become *us* – for good or ill. We must hold nothing in our minds that we do not want to hold within us permanently. The power of meditation is tremendous, and as we learn to harness this power to the Word of God, and use it daily to reconstruct our thought life, refocus our emotions and re-align our wills, it will not be long before others begin to see the characteristics of the Lord Jesus Christ appearing in us. The Living Word is revealed to us through the power of the written Word, held and meditated upon in our minds. Whatever you might forget through these studies, remember this – what you put into your mind today as meditation will come out tomorrow as fact.

Our secret meditations become us – for good or ill.

Father, from now on help me to apply the principle of meditation in every area of my life so that by the meditative Word and through the written Word, all around me may see the Living Word. Amen.